Stephanie Andrea Winkelbeiner

Quality of Life After Paediatric Stroke

Stephanie Andrea Winkelbeiner

Quality of Life After Paediatric Stroke

Five Year Follow-up Study of Affected Swiss Children

Human Sciences Series

Impressum / Imprint

Bibliografische Information der Deutschen Nationalbibliothek: Die Deutsche Nationalbibliothek verzeichnet diese Publikation in der Deutschen Nationalbibliografie; detaillierte bibliografische Daten sind im Internet über http://dnb.d-nb.de abrufbar.

Alle in diesem Buch genannten Marken und Produktnamen unterliegen warenzeichen-, marken- oder patentrechtlichem Schutz bzw. sind Warenzeichen oder eingetragene Warenzeichen der jeweiligen Inhaber. Die Wiedergabe von Marken, Produktnamen, Gebrauchsnamen, Handelsnamen, Warenbezeichnungen u.s.w. in diesem Werk berechtigt auch ohne besondere Kennzeichnung nicht zu der Annahme, dass solche Namen im Sinne der Warenzeichen- und Markenschutzgesetzgebung als frei zu betrachten wären und daher von jedermann benutzt werden dürften.

Bibliographic information published by the Deutsche Nationalbibliothek: The Deutsche Nationalbibliothek lists this publication in the Deutsche Nationalbibliografie; detailed bibliographic data are available in the Internet at http://dnb.d-nb.de.

Any brand names and product names mentioned in this book are subject to trademark, brand or patent protection and are trademarks or registered trademarks of their respective holders. The use of brand names, product names, common names, trade names, product descriptions etc. even without a particular marking in this works is in no way to be construed to mean that such names may be regarded as unrestricted in respect of trademark and brand protection legislation and could thus be used by anyone.

Coverbild / Cover image: www.ingimage.com

Verlag / Publisher:
AV Akademikerverlag
ist ein Imprint der / is a trademark of
OmniScriptum GmbH & Co. KG
Heinrich-Böcking-Str. 6-8, 66121 Saarbrücken, Deutschland / Germany
Email: info@akademikerverlag.de

Herstellung: siehe letzte Seite /
Printed at: see last page
ISBN: 978-3-639-64410-4

TABLE OF CONTENTS

Abbreviations

ADHD	Attention deficit and hyperactivity disorder
AIS1	Paediatric arterial ischaemic stroke
BSID-II	Bayley Scales of Infant Development
HRQoL	Health related quality of life
IQ	Intelligence quotient
K-ABC	Kaufman Assessment Battery
QoL	Quality of life
RF	Risk factor
SNPSR	Swiss Neuropaediatric Stroke Registry
TBI	Traumatic brain injury
VZV	Varicella zoster virus
WAIS	Wechsler Adult Intelligence Scale
WISC-III	Wechsler Intelligence Scale for Children

Introduction

Stroke in childhood is a life threatening medical condition with diverse impact on the future life of the child and its family. This paper focuses on pediatric arterial ischemic stroke (AIS1) and the quality of life (QoL) of affected children. Research suggests a relatively rare incidence of 2-13/100 000 children per year (Amlie-Lefond, Sébire, & Fullerton, 2008; Steinlin et al., 2005; Steinlin, 2012). However, it is important to identify and treat the ischemic lesion within the six-hour window as time has an impact on neurological and neuropsychological outcome (Steinlin et al., 2005). But not only time of diagnosis and intervention are critical factors for outcome, but also age at stroke. A lot of research studies found that early age at stroke is related to poorer overall outcome and an increased cognitive vulnerability (Amlie-Lefond et al., 2008 ; Everts et al., 2008 ; Ganesan et al., 2000 ; Pavlovic et al., 2006 ; Steinlin et al., 2005). This is in contrary to the traditional *early plasticity hypothesis* and supports the *early vulnerability hypothesis,* considering this age as the period of rapid development to be the most vulnerable (Westmacott, Askalan, Macgregor, Anderson, & DeVeber, 2009). Brain networks for higher cognitive functions are not yet fully developed (Pavlovic et al., 2006), thus the immature brain is limited in its capacity to compensate the ischemic lesions and to develop further higher-level cognitive skills (Cnossen et al., 2010; Westmacott et al., 2009).

Other factors mediating outcome are lesion characteristic such as lesion location, size and laterality. Concerning lesion location, Steinlin et al. (2004) found more handicaps in children suffering from a stroke in both cortical and subcortical regions. Additionally, Westmacott et al. (2009) found cortical infarcts in early childhood to be associated with poorer cognitive outcome due to a diminished capacity of the immature brain to reorganize successfully after such a lesion. Concerning lesion laterality findings are contradictory insofar as Amlie-Lefond et al. (2008) found bilateral infarcts to be linked to poorer overall outcome, but Gordon, Ganesan, Towell, and Kirkham (2002) found no influence on neuropsychological outcome as well as Everts et al. (2008) who found no influence of laterality on QoL. Lesion size is associated with outcome insofar that larger lesion volume leads to poorer functional outcome (De Schryver, Kappelle, Jennekens-Schinkel, & Boudewyn Peters, 2000; Gordon et al., 2002 ; Long, Anderson, Jacobs, Mackay, Leventer, Barnes, & Spencer-Smith, 2011).

Children who survive AIS1 are known to experience various health and psychological problems. Whereas neurological problems can be compensated more successfully, neuropsychological and behavioral problems remain life-long handicaps (Steinlin et al., 2004). This significantly influences the children's QoL (De Schryver et al., 2000; Everts et al., 2008; O'Keeffe, Ganesan, King, & Murphy, 2012; Steinlin et al., 2004) which is of great relevance to one's life (Friedfeld, Westmacott, MacGregor, & deVeber, 2011) and becomes more and more important in clinical research as a measure for outcome of paediatric stroke survivers (De Haan, Aaronson, Limburg, Hewer, & Van Crevel, 2012; Varni, Limbers, & Burwinkle, 2007a). Quality of life is "[…] an individual's satisfaction with all facets of life including physical, social, economic, and psychological wellbeing" (Upton, Lawford, & Eiser, 2008, p. 895). Health related quality of life (HRQoL), as a component of this concept, is a combination of health and QoL (Meral & Fidan, 2013). It can be defined as "[…] a psychological construct which describes the physical, mental, social, psychological, and functional aspects of wellbeing and function from a patient perspective" (Ravens-Sieberer & Bullinger, 1998, p. 399). From survival to QoL (Davis et al., 2007; Upton et al., 2008) and patient-reported outcome (Varni et al., 2007a) is a shift of focus in the clinical field. There are different findings concerning prognostic factors for QoL. Friefeld et al. (2011) found gender, age, and cognitive outcome to be linked to QoL. But in the study of O´Keeffe et al. (2012) no significant association between age, gender, and HRQoL could be found.

When it comes to evaluate QoL of children after stroke, parents and children tend to differ in their ratings (Christerson & Strömberg, 2010; Davis et al., 2007; Varni et al., 2007a). While children declare problems in social acceptance, parents report instability of moods and decreased social support from peers (Christerson & Strömberg, 2010; De Schryver et al., 2000; Everts et al., 2008). However, Eiser and Morse (2001) found good agreement (r>.50) for subdomains in physical activity, functioning, and symptoms, but poor agreement (r<.30) for emotional and social subdomains. This difference between self- and proxy-report is not due to the children to be too young. The study of Varni et al. (2007a) showed that children from the age of five years can reliably and validly report their HRQoL, but the agreement between self- and proxy-rating emerges with age as an important influence factor (Cremeens, Eiser, & Blades, 2001; Varni, Limbers, & Burwinkle, 2007b). The discordance between self- and proxy-report is due to different reasoning and different response styles (Davis et al., 2007). However, parents´ report should be included in the evaluation of the child´s HRQoL to complement the self-report as a secondary outcome measure (Davis et al., 2007; Varni et al., 2007a). The proxy-report is also a needed instrument in case the children are too young, too physically or mentally impaired, or too fatigued to complete a HRQoL questionnaire (Varni et al., 2007b).

The aim of this study was to collect data of paediatric stroke survivors concerning their QoL five years after stroke and to identify predictors of QoL such as age at stroke, gender, manual disabilities, IQ, and lesion characteristics. Based on current research it was hypothesized (1) that children after AIS1 have lower values in QoL compared to population norms, (2) that age at stroke, gender, cognitive outcome, motor impairments, and lesion characteristic such as location, laterality and size are associated with QoL, (3) that proxy-reports differ from self-report of the child´s QoL, and (4) that children needing special education after stroke have lower QoL outcome than children going to regular school.

Method

Subjects

Children living in Switzerland, who suffered from an ischaemic stroke or symptomatic sinus venous thrombosis since the year 2000 are registered in the *Swiss Neuropaediatric Stroke Registry* (SNPSR), a population-based multicenter registry of the University Children's Hospital in Bern, Switzerland. In this five year follow-up study children suffering from paediatric arterial ischaemic stroke (AIS1) between the year 2000 and 2007 were taken into account. Inclusion criteria were (1) AIS1, defined as "[…] focal neurological deficit of acute onset lasting at least 20 minutes and CT or MRT showing infarction in a localization consistent with neurological signs and symptoms" (Steinlin et al., 2005, p.91), (2) age of one months to 16 years at time of stroke, and (3) stroke occurring between the years 2000 and 2007.

Altogether 426 children were registered in the SNPSR by the time this study started. Eighty-eight children met the inclusion criteria, but not all could be included because 11 children died and data were not available for 15 children, who had moved and could not be contacted by post or telephone. Therefore a total of 62 children (40 males; 64.5%) remained and could be included in the study. Ages at stroke ranged from five months to 15.5 years (M=7.0, SD=5.1) and ages at assessment from 5.3 years to 20.6 years (M=12.2, SD=5.0). For more detailed demographic and neuropsychological data of the sample see Appendix A.

Patients were assigned to one of four age groups according to previous studies (Anderson et al., 2009; Pavlovic et al., 2006; Steinlin et al., 2005; Studer et al., 2013; Westmacott et al., 2010) and according to theoretical knowledge of brain development in childhood: (1) Early childhood (1 month-2:11 years), (2) preschool (3:0-5:11 years), (3) middle childhood (6:0-9:11 years), (4) late childhood (≥10 years). The groups are based on the fact that the process of synaptogenesis and thus the development of the immature brain take place in early childhood. This process of synaptic density is followed by a phase of no further significant change and decreases with the child getting older (Allman & Scott, 2011; Casey, Giedd, & Thomas, 2000; Everts et al., 2008; Pavlovic et al., 2006).

For evaluating stroke characteristics, patients were stratified by lesion location: cortical (involvement of white matter and cortical regions), subcortical (involvement of basal ganglia and/or thalamus and/or capsula interna), combined (involvement of cortical and subcortical regions, and infratentorial) brain stem and/or cerebellum. Patients were also stratified by laterality of stroke as left, right, or bilateral. At last, the sample was stratified by lesion size according to the previous study of Steinlin et al. (2005): large vascular territory (median, anterior, and posterior cerebral arteries) and small vascular territory (branches of the above vessels).

Measures

Quality of life and HRQoL was assessed with the self- and proxy-version of the Kidscreen-27 questionnaire (Ravens-Sieberer et al, 2001), a generic measurement for children and adolescents to identify risk for health problems. Twenty-seven items cover the five QoL subdomains which are briefly explained: *Physical wellbeing* represents the level of the child's/adolescent's physical activity, energy, and fitness, in which good physical wellbeing indicates little disabilities and disorders; *psychological wellbeing* represents positive emotions, satisfaction with life, and feeling emotionally balanced; *parents/autonomy* represents the child´s relationship with parents, the atmosphere at home, feelings of having enough age appropriate freedom, and degree of satisfaction with financial resources; s*ocial support* represents relationships with other children/adolescents and feelings of being accepted and integrated in peers; *school environment* represents the perceptions of cognitive capacity, learning, and concentration, and feelings about school. On a 5-point Likert scale one can rate importance and satisfaction (from 1=*not at all satisfied/important* to 5=*extremely satisfied/important*) (Bisegger, Cloetta, & the European Kidscreen Group, 2005; Davis et al., 2007; Meral & Fidan, 2013).

Demographic data and neurological characteristics were assessed with a frequently used questionnaire of the University Children´s Hospital in Bern, Switzerland. Included was the Abilhand Kids questionnaire (Arnould, Penta, Renders & Thonnard, 2004) to assess the degree of manual handicap respectively motor impairment in everyday life perceived by the patient. The higher the Abilhand Kids Score (0=*no manual handicap at all*), the greater the impairment.

Data concerning general intelligence were already assessed two years after the acute event and archived in the SNPSR data base. Assessment was done with age appropriate tests using Bayley Scales of Infant Development (BSID-II; Bayley, 1993) for children younger than 3 years, Kaufman Assessment Battery (K-ABC; Melchers & Preuss, 1991) for children between three and six years of age, and Wechsler Intelligence Scales (Wechsler Intelligence Scale for Children [WISC-III], Tewes, Rossmann, & Schallberger, 1999; Wechsler Adult Intelligence Scale [WAIS], Wechlser, 1992) for children aged six years or older. The results of the intelligence tests and the developmental test (BSID-II) are comparable providing that developmental tests also measure current cognitive functions of the child.

Procedure

Children suffering from AIS1 and registered in the SNPSR data base were examined again two years after the acute event of the stroke. Using age appropriate intelligence and developmental tests, cognitive abilities were assessed.

For this five year follow-up, the frequently used questionnaire of the University Children´s Hospital and the Kidscreen-27 self- and proxy-version (see Appendix B) were sent to the families of all children who had survived AIS1. The questionnaire of the University Children´s Hospital included questions concerning demographic data but also questions to assess motor abilities (Abilhand Kids Screen) and to evaluate attention deficits (ADHD concerned questions). Non-responders were contacted by phone and asked if they still wanted to take part at the research study and if so the questionnaire was sent again. The parents of 62 children returned the completed questionnaires. The two questionnaires returned after the end of April 2013 were not taken into account as data analysis had already started.

Statistical analysis

Data were analyzed using the Statistical Package for Social Sciences (SPSS) software version 18. Normal distribution was checked using Kolmogorov-Smirnov test. Distribution for lesion location, laterality, and size across the four age groups was tested with *Chi-Square* tests ($\chi2$). For comparing data of this sample with the Swiss-German norm-population one sample t-tests with a test value of 50 were performed with the Swiss T-values of the Kidscreen (M=50, SD=5) as a measure for QoL and HRQoL. It was decided to compare group means with only half a standard deviation because this already shows differences of middle effect size and implies certain noticeable values (Bisegger, Cloetta, & the European Kidscreen Group, 2005). With the Kidscreen-syntax Rasch-Scores were computed for each subdomain and transformed into T-Values; higher scores indicate higher QoL or HRQoL. In a first step, the sample was split up in the early described four age groups: One-way univariate analyses of variance (ANOVA) with *post hoc* Bonferroni correction were assessed to compare HRQoL in the four age groups. Additionally, multivariate ANOVA (MANOVA) with *post hoc* Bonferroni corrections was assessed to examine effects of age on QoL. In terms of searching for a relation between intelligence as well as motor abilities and QoL within the age groups, Pearson correlations were assessed. The two age groups, which differed the most were further tested using Mann-Whitney-U test. In a second step, data of the whole sample were analyzed searching for predictors of QoL and HRQoL: Therefore, the independent variables, age at stroke, gender, lesion characteristics (location, laterality, and size), motor impairment (Abilhand Kids Score), and IQ, were correlated with HRQoL using either Pearson or Spearman correlations. Laterality, location, and gender were selected for further analysis, because of the strongest correlation with HRQoL. Thereafter, a multiple linear regression was executed and male gender and bilateral stroke were found to be predictors. Subsequent, independent sample t-tests were assessed to see if HRQoL differs significantly within laterality and gender. In a third step, Kidscreen-data from parents were compared with those of the children to examine the degree of agreement between self- and proxy-report: Therefore, Pearson correlations were conducted. Because normal distribution of proxy-scores was not given, nonparametric Wilcoxon test was used to test if central tendency of the two connected samples (parents and children) differ significantly. It was further tested if proxy- and self-report differ less with increased age of the child, performing correlation analysis between the two reports within the four age groups. Additionally, t-Test for two connected samples was performed to see if groups differ less in the older age groups. At least, in a fourth step, children going to a special school after stroke were compared with those going to a regular school: independent sample t-tests for HRQoL and for QoL subdomains were assessed to search for a difference between the two groups. Because mean Abilhand Kids Score was much higher in the special school group, Mann Whitney U-Test was performed to examine differences in motor impairments in the two school groups. Also influences of IQ on QoL outcome were tested with independent sample t-test. Furthermore, Pearson respectively Spearman correlations were executed, in order to find relations between motor impairment as well as IQ and QoL or HRQoL.

Results

Sample characteristics

Analysis of the sample data (see Table 1) showed that 32 (51.6%) of 62 children suffered from left hemispheric (LH), 22 (35.5%) from right hemispheric (RH), and 8 (12.9%) from bilateral stroke. Data for lesion size was only available from 14 (22.6%) patients. Out of these 14 patients nine (64.3%) had a large lesion size and five (35.7%) had a small lesion size. Due to small cell numbers, lesion size was not further taken into account.

Table 1. Descriptive data of lesion characteristics

Lesion characteristics	N (%)	χ^2
Laterality		$\chi^2(9)=6.69, p=0.42; V=0.22$
- Left	32 (51.6%)	
- Right	22 (35.5%)	
- Bilateral	8 (12.9%)	
Size		$\chi^2(6)=6.74, p=0.35; V=0.23$
- Large	9 (14.5%)	
- Small	5 (8.1%)	
- unknown	48 (77.4%)	
Location		$\chi^2(6)=4.77, p=0.57; V=0.19$
- cortical	15 (24.2%)	
- subcortical	24 (38.7%)	
- combined cortical and subcortical	18 (29.0%)	
- infratentorial	5 (8.1%)	

Table 1. Detailed descriptive data concerning lesion characteristics of the sample.

Concerning lesion location, stroke was found to be in cortical regions in 15 (24.2%) children, in subcortical regions in 24 (38.7%) children, in combined subcortical and cortical regions in 18 (29.0%) children, and in infratentorial regions in 5 (8.1%) children. Due to small cell numbers infratentorial as a subgroup was also excluded from analysis. Results of χ^2 tests showed that lesion location ($\chi^2(6)=4.77$, $p=0.57$; $V=0.19$) and laterality ($\chi^2(9)=6.69$, $p=0.42$; $V=0.22$) were evenly distributed across the four age groups (For more detailed information see Appendix A).

Quality of life (QoL)

Data of Kidscreen-27 was not only available for all 62 children: Whereas 49 (79.03%) reports of physical wellbeing, psychological wellbeing, social support, and school environment were available, only 46 (74.19%) reports of parents/autonomy and HRQoL were available. Parents´ reports were also not complete: Fifty-six (90.32%) reports were available for physical wellbeing and psychological wellbeing, only 46 (74.19%) for parents/autonomy, 55 (88.71%) for social support and school environment, and 53 (85.48%) for HRQoL (see table 2 for more detailed information). In comparison with population norms, mean values of QoL and HRQoL lay within the normal range (Figure 1) which is in contrary to the first hypothesis. Although, social support was almost significantly decreased ($F(48)=-1.74$, $p=.088$) indicating a slight difference between our sample and norm population. Looking specifically to the four age groups, no significant difference of HRQoL ($F(3,42)=.188$, $p=.904$, $\eta^2= .013$) in the groups could be found. Moreover, no significant influence of age on the subdomains of QoL could be found ($F(1,44)=2.19$, $p=.08$, partial $\eta^2=.22$). Descriptive statistic showed though, that the youngest and the oldest children had the lowest means in three of five QoL subdomains compared to the other two age groups. While children in early childhood group had low average means in the subdomains of physical wellbeing ($M=47.73$, $SD=8.73$), parents/autonomy (M=46.31, SD=9.90), and social support (M=45.91, SD=9.94); children in late childhood group had low average means in the subdomains of physical wellbeing (M=47.95, SD=11.68), social support (M=46.91, SD=12.1), and school environment (M=48.76, SD=12.54). However, social support was low in all age groups (middle childhood M=45.42, SD=8.91; late childhood M=46.90, SD=12.10) except for preschool group (M=52.34, SD=8.14). Although the youngest children had the lowest HRQoL (M=49.91, SD=6.72), low average scores (M<45) in QoL subdomains were most often in late childhood.

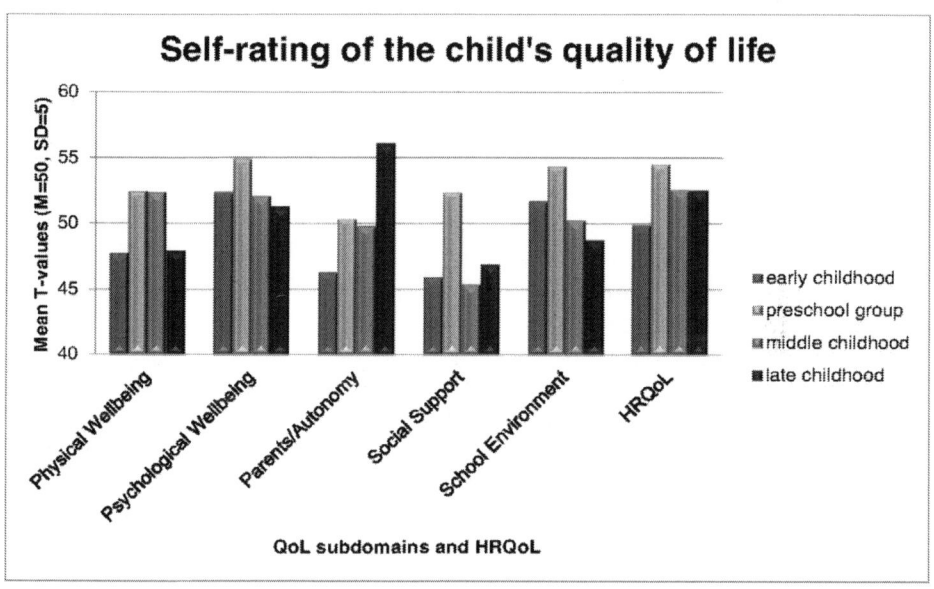

Figure 1. Mean values of each Kidscreen subdomain for all age groups. All mean T-values are within the normal range (M=50, SD=5), though parents/autonomy in late childhood group lies above average.

At time of testing, the sample had an overall IQ (M=97.43, SD=20.03) slightly under the normative population mean of 100 (SD=15). Noticeable, 16

(25.8%) children had an overall IQ below the normal range. Out of these 16 children, three (4.8%) had a low (M=70-79) and four (6.5%) an exceptionally low (M<69) IQ.

Table 2. Descriptive data of IQ, manual abilities and QoL

M (SD)	Total N	Early childhood	Preschool	Middle childhood	Late childhood
IQ	97.43 (20.03)	88.64(21.71)	105.60 (18.84)	93.90 (13,59)	101.25 (20.65)
Abilhand	3.13 (5.51)	6.06 (7.13)	2.69 (3.89)	2.67 (6.1)	1.23 (3.12)
QoLself					
PhW	49.82 (10.25)	47.74 (8.73)	48.22 (6.45)	51.17 (12.13)	51.44 (14.15)
PsyW	52.28 (9.64)	52.37 (9.61)	51.49 (8.51)	51.23 (10.66)	54.52 (11.74)
P/A	52.4 (13.76)	46.32 (9.90)	48.12 (12.25)	50.27 (10.67)	57.51 (17.45)
SS	47.40 (10.42)	45.92 (9.94)	51.62 (7.71)	46.09 (8.74)	46.85 (12.65)
SE	50.57 (10.74)	51.70 (6.64)	50.52 (10.31)	50.37 (10.94)	53.68 (14.58)
HRQOL	52.48 (11.44)	49.91 (6.72)	54.47 (8.85)	52.30 (13.05)	52.86 (13.81)
QoLproxy					
PhW	53.09 (14.3)	53.97(15.11)	47.48 (11.97)	49.48 (13.86)	42.83 (7.6)
PsyW	50.24 (13.36)	51.46(11.26)	43.48 (13.52)	51.84 (12.45)	52.37 (14.37)
P/A	51.23 (12.38)	48.95 (14.4)	42.61 (9.87)	51.12 (6.5)	52.1 (14.61)
SS	46.81 (13.54)	48.47(12.18)	46.33 (10.39)	41.92 (12.86)	43.89 (21.3)
SE	49.93 (10.62)	52.12 (9.35)	46.91 (8.3)	44.8 (10.40)	51.20 (11.95)
HRQOL	48.39 (12.44)	49.85(11.18)	45.87 (7.44)	53.46 (8.28)	49.83 (13.10)

Table 2. Mean values stratified by age for IQ, Abilhand Kids Screen (0= no manual handicaps), self- and proxy-report of QoL (PhW= Physical Wellbeing; PsW= Psychological wellbeing; P/A= Parents/autonomy; SS= Social support; SE= School environment; HRQoL=Health related quality of life).

In comparison with the other age groups, the youngest children had the lowest IQ (M=88.64, SD=21.71) although the oldest children had the lowest Performance IQ (M=95.74, SD=20.64). But beside that, no significant correlations between IQ and HRQoL could be found in the different age groups.

On the motor impairment measurement, the Abilhand Kids Screen, analysis revealed significantly higher Abilhand Kids Scores in early childhood group (M=6.06, SD=7.13) than in late childhood group (M=1.23, SD=3.12), indicating significantly more manual handicaps and motor impairment in younger children. Abilhand Kids Scores of children in preschool and middle childhood lay in between (preschool group M=2.60, SD=3.89; middle childhood M=2.67, SD=6.1). Apart from that, no significant correlations (p>.05) between Abilhand Kids Score and HRQoL could be found in the four age groups.

Predictors of QoL

Correlations´ analysis showed no significant correlations (p<.05) of HRQoL with one of the independent variables (age, IQ, motor impairment, gender, lesion characteristics). Nevertheless, gender, lesion laterality, and lesion location were analyzed more carefully within a multiple regression analysis hence their correlation with HRQoL were the highest (r≥.23). The model as a whole explained only one third of variance in children´s HRQoL, R^2=.32, $F(5,45)$=3.08, p=.02. The second hypothesis could therefore partially be confirmed, insofar as lesion size had to be excluded from analysis due to small cell numbers. Lesion locations as a predictor contributed only a non-significant amount of 3.7% to overall variance of HRQoL (cortical b=.22, $t(37)$=.96, p=.35; subcortical b=-.01, $t(37)$=-.03, p=.98; combined b=-.28, $t(37)$=-1.13, p=.27). However, male gender and bilateral lesion were found to be significant predictors. These two variables made a significant contribution to the outcome of HRQoL with 20% of variance explained by male gender (b=-.52, t(37)=-3.41, p=.00) and 9% of variance explained by bilateral lesion (b=-.36, t(37)=-2.33, p=.03).

Comparison of the population of males with the population of females showed that out of 62 children, 40 were males (64.5%) compared to 22 females (35.5%) who suffered from AIS1. Analysis with t-test revealed significant differences (Figure 2) between gender groups in the subdomain of parents/autonomy (t(22.63)=2.13, p=.04) and in the subdomain of social support (t(47)=2.76, p=.01).

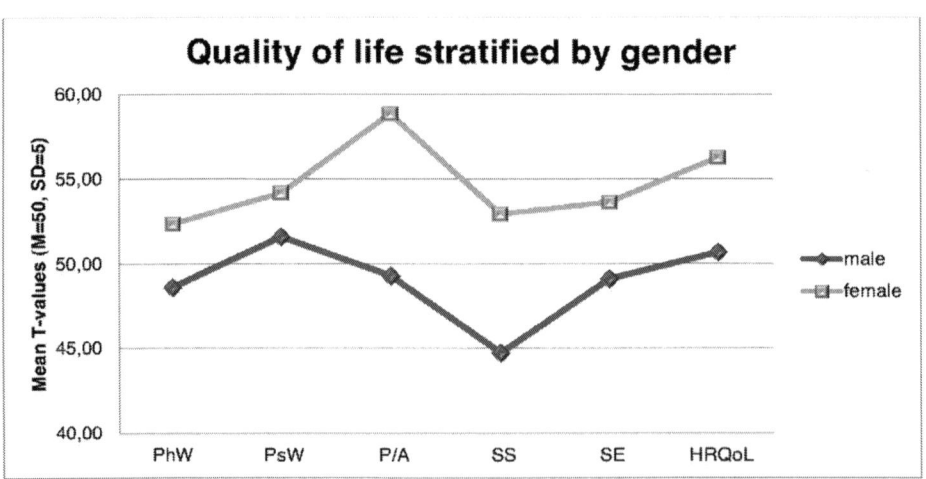

Figure 2. Reports from girls concerning their QoL are almost all in the higher average rage (M=50, SD=5), whereas boys' QoL values are in the average to low average range. PhW= Physical Wellbeing; PsW= Psychological wellbeing; P/A= Parents/autonomy; SS= Social support; SE= School environment; HRQoL=Health related quality of life.

Whereas male patients rated their QoL to be average and slightly below average in the subdomain of social support (M=44.73, SD=8.82), female patients rated their QoL to be more in the high average and even above average in the subdomain of parents/autonomy (M=58.86, SD=15.3) and in overall HRQoL (M=56.26, SD=13.73).

In terms of identifying predictors of QoL, laterality of stroke was analyzed next. This revealed that bilateral stroke was accompanied with lower QoL values (Figure 3). It appeared to be especially in the QoL subdomain of school environment in which laterality groups differed significantly from each other (t(47)=2.43, p=.02). While children after left hemispheric stroke reported QoL in school environment to be above average (M=54.63, SD=8.88), children after right hemispheric stroke reported it to be slightly below average (M=48.85, SD=10.77), and children with bilateral stroke reported it to be almost more than two standard deviations below average (M=41.87, SD=11.2).

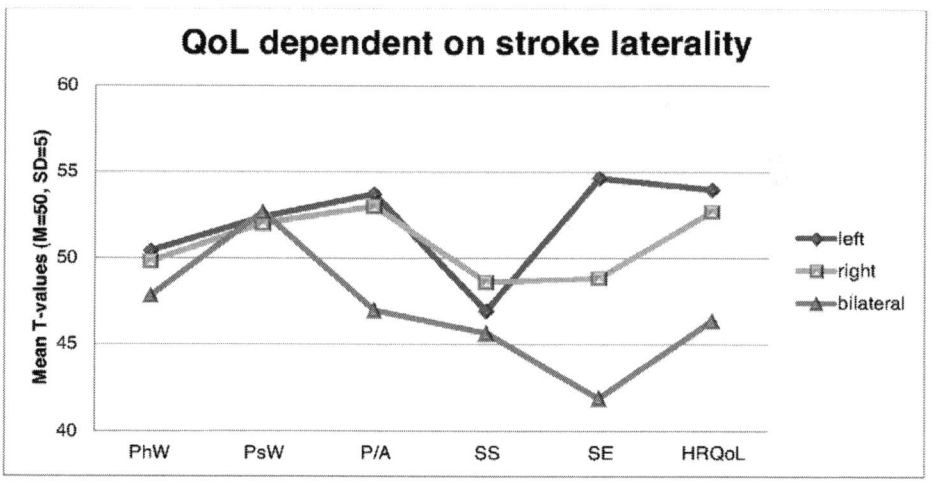

Figure 3. Mean scores of Kidscreen questionnaire of the whole sample stratified by lesion laterality (left, right, bilateral). All but one value lay within the normal range (M=50, SD=5). PhW= Physical wellbeing; PsW= Psychological wellbeing; P/A= Parents/autonomy; SS= Social support; SE= School environment; HRQoL= Health related quality of life.

Concerning the bilateral stroke group, a significant correlation between school environment and IQ could be found (r=.89, p=.02) but non with Abilhand Kids Score. For the other laterality groups no correlation with either IQ or Abilhand Kids Score was present. But for all that it is important to mention that only eight (12.90%) of the total 62 children had a bilateral stroke.

Relationship between self- and proxy-report

Concerning self- and proxy-report, analysis between parents and children rating the child's QoL showed significant correlations (p<.05). There were strong associations between all QoL subdomains which led to the rejection of the third hypothesis proclaiming that self- and proxy-report differ from each other (Figure 4). Good agreement (r≥.50) was found for physical wellbeing (r(41)=.54, p=.00), psychological wellbeing (r(41)=.50, p=.00), social support (r(41)=.69, p=.00), and school environment (r(41)=.72, p=.00), but poor agreement (r≥.30) for parents/autonomy (r(37)=.34, p=.03). Although all T values were in the average range for both groups, ratings differed most in the subdomain of physical wellbeing with parents rating their children to be above average (M=53.09, SD=14.23) but children rated their QoL in this subdomain to be almost average (M=49.82, SD=10.25). Furthermore, self- and proxy-rating differed significantly (p<.02) in overall HRQoL: Parents rated their children's HRQoL to be slightly under average (M=48.39, SD=12.44), while children thought their HRQoL to be slightly above average (M=52.48, SD=11.44). Parents tended to rate social support (M=46.81, SD=13.54) and school environment (M=49.93, SD=10.62) the lowest, whereas children rated physical wellbeing (M=49.82, SD=10.25) and social support (M=47.40, SD=10.42) the lowest. Compared with parents of children with no disabilities, a trend towards (t(54)=-1.75, p=.09) lower rating of social support by parents of this sample could be found.

In terms of investigating influence of age on the level of agreement between parents' and children's ratings, correlations between self- and proxy-report were analyzed. This revealed that within the late childhood group reports correlated significantly high (r≥.50, p<.05) in four of six domains, namely physical wellbeing (r=.56, p=.25), social support (r=.71, p=.00), school environment (r=.91, p=.00), and HRQoL (r=.63, p=.02). In contrast to that, in early childhood group only one significant correlation between self- and proxy-report could be found, namely in the subdomain of social support (r=.84, p=.02).

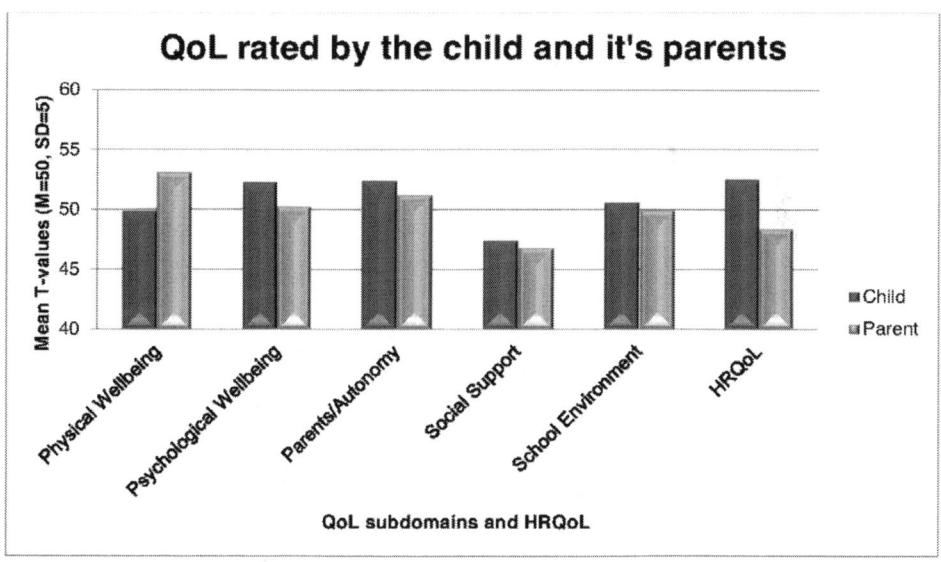

Figure 4. Parents' and children's report of the child's QoL, represented by the five Kidscreen subdomains and the overall HRQoL. All mean T-values lay within the normal range (M=50, SD=5). Noticeable that the subdomain social support was rated the lowest by both children and parents.

Effects of stroke on school and professional life

In order to search for effects on school and professional life, the sample was divided in children needing special education and children going to regular school. Out of 62 children, 13 (20.97%) needed special schooling, but most could be educated in mainstream schools (49, 79.03%). This subsample (special school group) consisted of five girls (38.5%) and eight boys (61.5%) who were between 5.24 and 20.20 years of age at assessment (M=10.38, SD=5.27). Age at assessment is important as so far as school gets more challenging with every grade and cognitive deficits as well as other handicaps increase with greater demands.

In concordance with the last hypothesis, the two groups differed significantly (t(44)=-2.08, p=.04) in their ratings (Figure 5). Children going to special school rated their HRQoL more often as under average (57.1%) compared to only six (15.4%) children in regular school. On the single QoL subdomains, groups differed significantly in their rating of parents/autonomy (t(13.35)=-2.48, p=.03) and a trend towards a difference in physical wellbeing between the groups was noticeable (t(47)=-1.75, p=.09). With regard to cognitive outcome, children in special school differed significantly in their IQ from children in regular school (t(52)=-2.52, p=.02). Those children in special school had a mean IQ more than one standard deviation below average (M=82.78, SD=28.04), whereas children in regular school lay within average (M=100.36, SD=16.96). However, IQ did not significantly (p>.05) correlate with HRQoL.

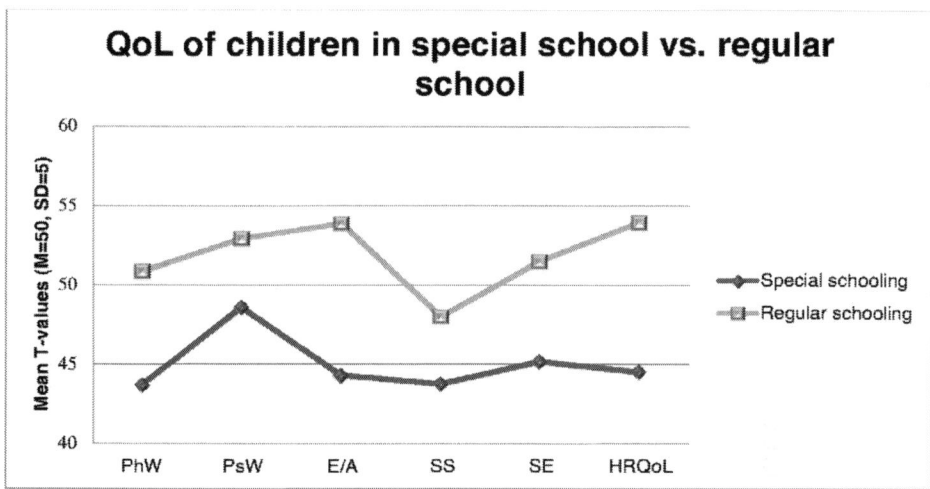

Figure 5. Self-report of children´s QoL measured with Kidscreen-27 questionnaire. Mean T-values of children going to regular school are in the average range (M=50, SD=5), whereas values of children needing special education are significantly lower and all but one under average. PhW= Physical wellbeing; PsW= Psychological wellbeing; P/A= Parents/autonomy; SS= Social support; SE= School environment; HRQoL= Health related quality of life.

Discussion

The aim of the present study was to gain further insight in the development of QoL in children who suffered from stroke. Influencing factors of QoL such as age at stroke, gender, IQ, motor impairments, and lesion characteristics were investigated, self- and proxy report of children´s QoL were compared, and children needing special education after stroke were analyzed to find differences in QoL compared to children going to regular school after stroke.

Concerning the first hypothesis, recent studies (Everts et al., 2008; Friefeld et al., 2011; O´Keeffe et al., 2012; Steinlin, Roelin, & Schroth, 2004) showed that children after AIS1 had lower values in QoL compared to healthy population. This hypothesis could not be confirmed in this study. Instead, results of the Kidscreen-27 questionnaire related to QoL and HRQoL fell within the normal range. However, these findings confirm other studies (Cnossen et al., 2010; De Schryver et al., 2000; Gordon et al., 2002) where children were found to experience good long-term QoL after AIS1. Although, this was not true for the subdomain social support, in which an almost significant value indicated a trend towards a difference to norm-population insofar, that children after stroke feel less supported by peers. This is in concordance with recent studies (Everts et al., 2008; Friedfeld, Yeboah, Jones, & deVeber, 2004; Friefeld et al., 2011) where QoL related to psychosocial domains was found to be the most problematic and related to physical domains to be the least problematic. Apart from that, average satisfaction of the child with its QoL was attributed in the study of Steinlin et al. (2004) to the acute and life threatening event of a stroke in early years of life which is still in mind of patients and parents when confronted with the questions of the Kidscreen-27. Furthermore, research

24

about this phenomenon, known as *disability paradox*, implies that people beside significant and persistent health problems can still be satisfied with their lives. High QoL scores could be a consequence or rather a "secondary gain" (Albrecht & Devlieger, 1999) of the individual adapting to the new conditions and trying to make sense of them. In the process of that, individuals reinterpret their lives and might find an enriched meaning in their role in life beside their disability (Albrecht & Devlieger, 1999). Another explanation for good QoL of patients "[...] may be attributable to well-functioning families, good support from schools, satisfactory rehabilitation and community services minimizing the experience of the disability" (Christerson & Strömberg, 2010, p.1655).

Focusing on predictors of QoL revealed that neuropsychological outcome such as QoL and HRQoL was more dependent on male gender and bilaterality of lesion than on location of stroke, IQ, or motor impairments. The predictive model accounted only for one third of variance of QoL which led to the conclusion that there are other factors not yet identified which might account to the proportion of unexplained variance. Thus, the findings confirmed only partially the second hypothesis which implied that age at stroke, gender, cognitive outcome, motor impairments, and lesion characteristic are associated with QoL. This is an interesting finding though and in contrary to previous studies (Friefeld et al., 2011; O´Keeffe et al., 2012), where cognitive and motor deficits were strongly linked to QoL. Children are more handicapped with either cognitive deficits or motor impairments and are therefore more limited in their participation in daily life (Friefeld et al., 2011; O´Keeffe et al., 2012). Therefore, one would expect them to be less satisfied with their lives and would, as a consequence, rate their QoL lower. But for this association no evidence was found in this study. However, future research on this sample should include neurological severity beside IQ and Abilhand Kids Score as another objective measure of the child´s wellbeing to correlate with QoL.

Concerning gender as a predictor for QoL, analysis showed, concordant with previous studies (Pavlovic et al., 2006; Steinlin et al., 2004), a predominance of male patients in this sample. However, there is no explanation for this predominance available yet (Steinlin, 2012). The association between gender and QoL was also evident in previous studies (Cnossen et al., 2010; Friefeld et al., 2004; Friefeld et al., 2011). Comparison between males and females in this sample revealed that male patients rated their QoL significantly lower than female patients. Furthermore, females and males differed the most in their rating of parents/autonomy and social support. Females were most satisfied with parents/autonomy which indicates a good and supportive relationship with parents and the percipience of autonomy and availability of financial resources. Whereas social support was rated the lowest by males, which could be a sign for non-satisfying relationships with friends or the male´s feeling of not being integrated or accepted by peers.

The findings concerning lesion characteristics revealed no predictive value of lesion location for QoL, consistent with previous studies (Amlie-Lefond et al., 2008; Ganesan et al., 2000; Pavlovic et al., 2006; Steinlin et al., 2004). Besides the results of Gordon et al. (2002) and Everts et al. (2008) who found no link between laterality and QoL, lesion laterality was found in this study to be a predictor of QoL. Children who suffered from bilateral stroke had lower values in QoL than children who suffered from stroke in either left or right hemisphere. This finding veers towards results of Amlie-Lefond et al. (2008) who found an association between bilateral infarct and poorer overall outcome. Everts et al. (2008), who found no such relation, came to the conclusion that stroke had no direct impact on cognitive outcome which was due to the fact that the brain networks are widespread and bilateral and therefore might compensate for the lost functions. But if both hemispheres are affected from stroke the capacity to compensate might be limited, deficits might get more noticeable, and this might then has an impact on QoL. Children suffering from bilateral stroke had significantly lower values in ever subdomain of QoL except for the subdomain of psychological wellbeing. In this specific subdomain, children independently of lesion laterality had almost the same average levels of QoL. This is an interesting finding given that previous studies (Everts et al., 2008; Friedfeld et al., 2004; Friefeld et al., 2011) found QoL related to psychosocial domains to be the domain with less satisfying outcome. Another interesting finding is the great variability in mean scores of the subdomain school environment between all three laterality groups. Whereas children suffering from left hemispheric stroke reported their QoL in school environment to be in the high average range, children after right hemispheric stroke reported it to be slightly under average, and children with bilateral stroke reported it to be below average. This could be a sign for the less favourable outcome in children with bilateral stroke which shows up especially in school environment. Friefeld et al. (2004) also found school to be the lowest rated subdomain of QoL. An explanation for this might be the limited capacity of the brain to compensate bilateral lesions which affect cognitive functioning as well as motor abilities. Approving for this explanation, results showed a significant and positive correlation between IQ and satisfaction with school environment, but none for Abilhand Kids Score and school environment. These astonishing results implicate that only the level of cognitive functioning had an impact on QoL in school environment and not manual handicaps. O'Keeffe et al. (2012) also found cognitive difficulties to be associated with poorer HRQoL, but they also found higher levels of executive dysfunctions in children with lower HRQoL as well. More research is needed to investigate the subgroup of children with bilateral stroke further and to find factors influencing their QoL. Lesion size could not be included in analysis due to small cell number and therefore no statement of that independent variable can be made.

In terms of identifying impact of age on QoL, results indicated no significant difference between the four age groups concerning HRQoL and also no effect of age on QoL. This is in concordance with findings of O´Keeffe et al. (2012) and Tham et al. (2009). However, looking more carefully to the Kidscreen data, young children were found to be less satisfied with their QoL in three of five subdomains, namely physical wellbeing, parents/autonomy, and social support. Additionally, these children had the lowest HRQoL compared to the other age groups. The results of similar studies (Amlie-Lefond et al., 2008; Ganesan et al., 2000) tend to go in the same direction as younger children were found to have a worse prognosis compared to older children and were more vulnerable to poor outcome. Interestingly, the youngest children did not rate school environment to be less satisfying, although their IQ was the lowest compared to the other age groups. This age group is thought to have the worst cognitive outcome because the young brain is most vulnerable to injuries (Everts et al., 2008). The immature brain is not yet fully developed and damage to brain networks interferes with later development of higher cognitive functions. Furthermore, the extent of neural network development and the existent abilities at time of stroke are important for outcome and reorganization (Pavlovic et al., 2006) and are less in younger children than in older. However, consistent with findings of Friefeld et al. (2011), beside the youngest children also the oldest children in this study were found to be less satisfied with QoL. They had low values in the subdomains of physical wellbeing, social support, and school environment. Concerning physical wellbeing, this subdomain was rated low by early childhood group as well. This is an astonishing finding given that children in late childhood had less motor deficits than all other children and still rated their physical wellbeing as under average. However, no significant association between motor impairment and HRQoL could be found. Further analysis revealed that there was no significant association between motor impairments and HRQoL.

Beside the low ratings of physical wellbeing, all age groups except the preschool group reported the subdomain of social support to be less satisfying. The low values in this subdomain could be due to the experience of being handicapped or limited in motor abilities or being not on the same developmental level as peers. This subdomain is known to be of greatest concern to the children (Everts et al., 2008), especially in the period of life when peers get more important and children detach more and more from family. Findings like these show the importance of support and integration help for families and children after stroke. Further research is needed to find an explanation why children in preschool group were none the less more satisfied with social support than all other children.

The finding that school environment was less satisfying for children in late childhood group could be accounted to the low average of Performance IQ in this group. In a similar vein, Cnossen et al. (2010) reported long-term cognitive impairments after ischemic stroke to be caused by "a failure to develop adequate new neurological pathways" (p.399). Although no significant relation between IQ and HRQoL could be found within the age groups, this phenomenon, known as *growing into deficit,* could still be an explanation for decreased perception of QoL in older children given that impaired cognitive functions have an impact on various parts of life. Concerning results of IQ in the sample, a confounder might be the fact that comparison of developmental quotients with intelligence quotients is limited. In summary, laterality and gender were found to be predictors of QoL as well as age, although not significantly.

Concerning the third hypothesis, comparison between parents´ and child´s report on children´s QoL revealed strong associations between self- and proxy-rating. This led to the rejection of this hypothesis, proclaiming a difference in the two reports. In the study of O´Keeffe et al. (2012) this was assumed to be due to more communication and sharing of information between persons concerned. This leads to higher agreement between children and parents about the child´s needs and wellbeing. In concordance with results of Eiser and Morse (2001) good agreement was found for physical activity, but on contrary to Eiser and Morse´s findings, agreement for emotional and social subdomains was found to be good in this study. Only a poor agreement for parents/autonomy was present, which indicates different perception of parents and children on their relationship, the atmosphere at home, feelings of having enough age appropriate freedom, or degree of satisfaction with financial resources. This could be due to a limited insight of parents into their child´s life and to a different access of parents to information about the child (Jovic, Locker, & Guyatt, 2003). It is probably more difficult for parents to rate for example if their child felt fair treated by its parents than to rate for example if their child was full of energy (item of physical wellbeing). As in previous studies, for both parents and children, the effect of stroke on social support was of greatest concern (Everts et al., 2008), followed by its impact on school (Friefeld et al, 2004) from parents´ point of view and on physical wellbeing from children´s point of view. In the subdomain of social support, parents in this study differed significantly in their ratings from parents of healthy children. The fact that social support was rated the lowest by both parents and children leads to the assumption that families feel their child not being supported properly by friends and peers which seems to be especially after the acute event of a stroke. Whereas the fact that physical wellbeing was rated low by children can be accounted to the high frequency of impaired sensory-motor function caused by the ischemic lesion (Friefeld et al., 2012). This evaluation by children and parents shows the expansive and detrimental impact of stroke on children's HRQoL, consistent with recent findings (Cnossen et al., 2010; Friefeld et al., 2004; Gordon et al., 2002; O'Keeffe et al., 2012). As shown in previous studies (Cremeens et al., 2001; Varni et al., 2007b), agreement between parents' and children's report emerge with age. Therefore age is assumed to be an important predictor for the level of agreement between self- and proxy-report of QoL.

The findings on children who need special education after stroke are concordant with findings of O'Keeffe et al. (2012) insofar, as 21% of children needed special schooling and had lower QoL scores than children going to regular school after stroke. However, in the study of De Schryver et al. (2000) almost a third needed special education. The two school groups (special school group and regular school group) differed significantly in their ratings of QoL and HRQoL and children in special school more often rated their HRQoL to be under average. These results confirm the last hypothesis that children going to special school after stroke have a lower QoL than children going to regular school after stroke. The association between special educational needs and lower HRQoL was also found by O'Keeffe et al. (2012). One explanation for this might be the presence of more disabilities or greater handicaps in the children's daily live. Another explanation might be that children after stroke need to relearn skills disturbed by stroke, to keep up with ongoing challenges of school, to adapt to handicaps, and to acquire new skills which were not yet developed when stroke occurred (Friefeld et al., 2012). Altogether, these are big challenges and might overstrain the child sometimes which then leads to lower satisfaction with life. However, although children with special education had significantly more motor impairments than children in regular school, no association to either QoL or HRQoL could be found. This was the same for the IQ: children in special school had significantly lower IQ values, with more than one standard deviation below average, and were therefore more cognitively handicapped than children in regular school. Nevertheless, no association between cognitive impairment and QoL could be found either. This surprising finding, that neither motor impairment nor cognitive deficits influenced QoL in these children, might be contributed to good integration and support from the school system. However, further research is needed to investigate influencing factors on HRQoL in this subgroup of stroke survivors.

Finally, it is important to consider the limitations to this study. First of all, data of Kidscreen questionnaires were not completely filled in for all children and socio economic status of parents was not available. The socio economic status would have contributed to outcome insofar as socioeconomic and demographic factors are supposed to influence outcome in certain ways (Denis, 2000). A larger sample size would have allowed more detailed analysis, especially for investigations of predictors of QoL. And although sample size was considerable, given the rareness of AIS1, sometimes subgroups were still too small to be taken into statistical analysis. Secondly, another factor which might limit the results of this study is the use of different tests such as intelligence and developmental tests to examine cognitive outcome. This was due to the need for age appropriate testing, but limited the value of results when comparing for example the subgroup early childhood, tested with a developmental test, with the subgroup late childhood, tested with an IQ test.

Thirdly, self-ratings of the children's QoL might be limited by the fact that the Kidscreen questionnaire is constructed for children at the age of eight. But there is increasing evidence about children younger than eight being able to "[...] use rating scales, can use common response terms, and can understand and interpret underlying concepts, and therefore should be able to assess their own HRQoL" (Upton et al., 2008, p. 869). Furthermore, research showed (Varni et al., 2007b) that children from the age of five years reliably and validly rate their HRQoL. Additionally, parent proxy-report can be taken as an outcome measure when the child is too young or too handicapped to fill in the questionnaire itself (Varni et al., 2007b).

Further research is needed to investigate which factors decrease self-report of QoL in children needing special schooling compared to children going to regular school. Finally, it would be interesting to study this sample again in a few years and re-analyze their development and present QoL.

Conclusion

To summarize the results gained from this study it was shown that quality of life is an important outcome measure for both parents and children when it comes to evaluate outcome following paediatric AIS. In terms of QoL, using Swiss norms, this study could not find significant differences in lowered QoL following AIS1 although the youngest children thought their QoL to be lower in more subdomains of QoL than in any other age group of this sample. Predictors of HRQoL were found to be gender and lesion laterality although age at stroke also had an influence on QoL ratings. This study could show that parent proxy-report and child self-report were strongly associated and differed only in the subdomain of physical wellbeing and overall HRQoL. Also lower levels of QoL were found in children needing special education after stroke. More follow-up studies are necessary to monitor longer-term outcome and to improve support of children who survived AIS1 and their families.

References

Albrecht, G. L., & Devlieger, P. J. (1999). The disability paradox: high quality of life against all odds. *Social science & medicine, 48*(8), 977-988.

Allman, C. & Scott, R. B. (2011). Neurological sequelae following pediatric stroke: A nonlinear model of age at lesion effects. *Child Neuropsychology, iFirst,* 1-11.

Anderson, V., Spencer-Smith, M., Leventer, R., et al. (2009). Childhood brain insult: Can age at insult help us predict outcome? *Brain, 132,* 45-56.

Amelie-Lefond, C., Sébire, G., & Fullerton, H. J. (2008). Recent developments in childhood arterial ischaemic stroke. *Lancet Neurol, 7,* 425-435.

Arnould, C., Penta, M., Renders, A. & Thonnard, J.-L. (2004). ABILHAND-kids: a measure of manual ability in children with cerebral palsy. *Neurol, 63,*1045-52.

Bayley N. Bayley Scale for Infant Development (BSID-II), 2nd ed. San Antonio: The Psychological Corporation, 1993.

Bortz, J., & Lienert, G. A. (1998). *Kurzgefasste Statistik für die klinische Forschung. Ein praktischer Leitfaden für die Analyse kleiner Stichproben.* Berlin: Springer.

Bisegger, C., Cloetta, B. & die europäische Kidscreengruppe (2005). Kidscreen: Fragebogen zur Erfassung der gesundheitsbezogenen Lebensqualität von Kindern und Jugendlichen. Manual der deutschsprachigen Versionen für die Schweiz. Bern: Abteilung für Gesundheitsforschung des Instituts für Sozial- und Präventivmedizin der Universität.

Casey, B. J., Giedd, J. N., & Thomas, K. M. (2000). Structural and functional brain development and its relation to cognitive development. *Biological psychology, 54*(1), 241-257.

Christerson, S., & Strömberg, B. (2010). Stroke in Swedish children II: long-term outcome. *Acta Paediatrica, 99*, 1650-1656.

Cnossen, M., Aarsen, F., Van Den Akker, S., Danen, R., Appel, I., Steyerberg, E.,& Catsman-Berrevoets, C. (2010). Paediatric arterial ischaemic stroke: Functional outcome and risk factors. *Developmental Medicine and Child Neurology, 52*, 394–399.

Cremeens, J., Eiser, C., & Blades, M. (2006). Factors influencing agreement between child self-report and parent proxy-reports on the Pediatric Quality of Life Inventory™ 4.0 (PedsQL™) Generic Core Scales. *Health and quality of life outcomes, 4*(58), 1-8.

Davis, E., Nicolas, C., Waters, E., Cook, K., Gibbs, L., Gosch, A., & Ravens-Sieberer, U. (2007). Parent-proxy and child self-reported health-related quality of life: using qualitative methods to explain the discordance. *Quality of Life Research, 16*(5), 863-871.

De Haan, R. D., Aaronson, N., Limburg, M., Hewer, R. L., & Van Crevel, H. (1993). Measuring quality of life in stroke. *Stroke, 24*(2), 320-327.

Dennis, M. (2000). Developmental plasticity in children: the role of biological risk, development, time, and reserve. *Journal of Communication Disorders, 33*(4), 321-332.

De Schryver, L. M., Kappelle, L. J., Jennekens-Schinkel, A., & Boudewyn Peters, A. C. (2000). Prognosis of ischemic stroke in childhood: A long-term follow-up study. Developmental Medicine and Child Neurology, 42, 313–318.

Eiser, C., & Morse, R. (2001). Can parents rate their child's health-related quality of life? Results of a systematic review. *Quality of Life Research*, *10*(4), 347-357.

Everts, R., Pavlovic, J., Kaufmann, F., Uhlenberg, B., Seidel, U., Nedeltchev, K., Perrig, W., & Steinlin, M. (2008). Cognitive functioning, behavior, and quality life after stroke in childhood. *Child Neuropsychology, 14,* 323–338.

Friefeld, S., Yeboah, O., Jones, J.E., & deVeber, G. (2004). Health-related quality of life and its relationship to neurological outcome in child survivors of stroke. *CNS Spectr, 9,* 465–75.

Friefeld, S., Westmacott, R., MacGregor, D., & deVeber, G. (2011). Predictors of Quality of Life in Pediatric Survivors of Arterial Ischemic Stroke and Cerebral Sinovenous Thrombosis. *Journal of Child Neurology, 26 (9),* 1186-1192.

Ganesan, V., Hogan, A., Shack, H., Gordon, A., Isaacs, E., & Kirkham, F. J. (2000). Outcome after ischemic stroke in childhood. *Developmental Medicine Child Neurology, 42,* 455–461.

Gordon, A.L., Ganesan, V., Towell, A., & Kirkham, F.J. (2002). Functional outcome following stroke in children. *Journal of Child Neurology, 17,* 429–434.

Long, B., Anderson, V., Jacobs, R., Mackay, M., Leventer, R., Barnes, C., & Spencer-Smith, M. (2011). Executive function following child stroke: The impact of lesion size. *Developmental neuropsychology*, *36*(8), 971-987.

Melchers P, Preuss U. Kauman Assessment Battery for Children (K-ABC). Deutschsprachige Fassung. Frankfurt am Main: Sweets & Zeitlinger, 1991.

Meral, A., & Fidan, R. (2013). The Examination of Psychometric Properties of KIDSCREEN-Short Version on Children with Autism in Turkey. *International Journal on New Trends in Education and Their Implications*, 4 (2), 151-159.

O'Keeffe, F., Ganesan, V., King, J., & Murphy, T. (2012). Quality-of-life and psychosocial outcome following childhood arterial ischaemic stroke. *Brain Injury*, *26*(9), 1072-1083.

Pavlovic, J., Kaufmann, F., Boltshauser, E., Capone Mori, A., Gubser Mercati, D., et al. (2006). Neuropsychological problems after pediatric stroke: Two year follow-up of Swiss children. *Neuropediatrics, 37(1)*, 13–19.

Ravens-Sieberer, U. & Bullinger, M. (1998). Assessing health-related quality of life in chronically ill   children with the German KINDL: First psychometric and content analysis results. *Quality of Life Research*, 7, 399–407.

Ravens-Sieberer, U., Gosch, A., Abel, T., Auquier, P., Bellach, B. M., Bruil, J., ...the European KIDSCREEN Group. (2001). Quality of life in children and adolescents: A European public health perspective. *Soziale Praventiv Medizin, 46*, 297–302.

Steinlin, M., Roelin, K., & Schroth, G. (2004). Long-term follow-up after stroke in childhood. *European Journal of Pediatrics, 163*, 245–250.

Steinlin, M., Pfister, I., Pavlovic, J., Boltshauser, E., Capone, M., Mori, A., ...Weissert, M. (2005). The first three years of the Swiss Neuropediatric Stroke Registry (SNPSR): A population-based study of incidence, symptoms and risk factors. *Neuropediatrics, 36*, 90–97.

Steinlin, M. (2012). A clinical approach to arterial ischemic childhood stroke: increasing knowledge over the last decade. *Neuropediatrics, 43*(01), 001-009.

Studer, M., Boltshauser, E., Capone Mori, A., Datta, A.N., Fluss, J., Mercati, D., ... Steinlin, M. (in press). When stroke strikes early – impacting factors for cognitive outcome in pediatric stroke.

Tham, E. H., Tay, S. K., & Low, P. S. (2009). Factors predictive of outcome in childhood stroke in an Asian population. *Annals Academy of Medicine Singapore*, *38*(10), 876-881.

Tewes U, Rossmann P, Schallberger U. Hamburg-Wechsler-Intelligenztest für Kinder (HAWIK-III). Bern: Huber, 1999.

Upton, P., Lawford, J., & Eiser, C. (2008). Parent-child agreement across child health-related quality of life instruments: a review of the literature. *Quality of Life Research* 17, 895-913.

Varni, J. W., Limbers, C. A., & Burwinkle, T. M. (2007a). How young can children reliably and validly self-report their health-related quality of life?: An analysis of 8,591 children across age subgroups with the PedsQL™ 4.0 Generic Core Scales. *Health and quality of life outcomes*, *5*(1), 1-13.

Varni, J. W., Limbers, C. A., & Burwinkle, T. M. (2007b). Parent proxy-report of their children's health-related quality of life: an analysis of 13,878 parents' reliability and validity across age subgroups using the PedsQL™ 4.0 Generic Core Scales. *Health and Quality of Life Outcomes*, *5*(1), 1-10.

Wechsler, D. (1992). *The Wechsler Intelligence Scale for Children-III*. London: Psychological Corporation.

Westmacott, R., Askalan, R., Macgregor, D., Anderson, P., & DeVeber, G. (2009). Cognitive outcome following unilateral arterial ischaemic stroke in childhood: Effects of age at stroke and lesion location. *Developmental Medicine and Child Neurology, 52*, 386–393.

Appendix A. Patient characteristics, stroke characteristics and neuropsychological measures

Parameter	Early childhood	Middle childhood	Preschool	Late Childhood	Total
N	18	10	12	22	62
Age at stroke onset, M (SD)	1.1 (0.6)	4.0 (0.7)	7.8 (1.2)	12.8 (1.7)	7.00 (5.05)
Age at stroke onset, *range* (years)	0.5-2.5	3.5-5.5	6.0-9.5	10-15.5	0.5 – 15.5
Age at assessment, M (SD)	6.3 (0.9)	9.2 (0.8)	12.9 (1.3)	17.9 (1.7)	12.2 (5.0)
Age at assessment, *range* (years)	5.3-8.0	8.3-10.3	10.8-14.6	14.7-20.6	5.3–20.6
Sex, n (%) males	11 (61.1%)	8 (80.0%)	9 (75%)	12 (54.5%)	40 (64.5%)
Risk factors, n (%)					
Traumatic brain injury (TBI)	1 (5.6%)	2 (20.0%)	1 (8.3%)	2 (9.1%)	6 (9.7%)
Infection	8 (44.4%)	5 (50.0%)	7 (58.3%)	8 (36.4%)	28 (45.2%)

- Varicella zoster virus	4 (22.2%)	4 (40.0%)	3 (25.0%)	7 (31.8%)	18 (29.0%)
- fever	2 (11.1%)	1 (10.0%)	0 (0.0%)	0 (0.0%)	3 (4.8%)
Migraine	1 (5.6%)	0 (0.0%)	0 (0.0%)	2 (9.1%)	3 (4.8%)
Unknown/Non identified	8 (44.4%)	3 (30.0%)	4 (33.3%)	10 (45.5%)	25 (40.3%)

Neurological diagnosis pre stroke, n (%)

Developmental retardation	2 (11.1%)	1 (10.0%)	0 (0.0%)	1 (4.5%)	4 (6.5%)
Learn disabilities	0 (0.0%)	0 (0.0%)	0 (0.0%)	3 (13.6%)	3 (4.8%)
ADHD	0 (0.0%)	1 (10.0%)	1 (8.3%)	0 (0.0%)	2 (3.2%)
Epilepsy	2 (11.1%)	0 (0.0%)	0 (0.0%)	1 (4.5%)	3 (4.8%)
Disorder of speech development	0 (0.0%)	1 (10.0%)	1 (8.3%)	0 (0.0%)	2 (3.2%)
Unknown/Non identified	14 (77.8%)	3 (70.0%)	10 (83.3%)	17 (77.3%)	48 (77.4%)

Localization, *n* (%)

Cortical	3 (16.7%)	3 (30.0%)	3 (25.0%)	6 (27.3%)	15 (24.2%)
Subcortical	8 (44.4%)	5 (50.0%)	5 (41.7%)	6 (27.3%)	24 (38.7%)
Infratentorial	2 (11.1%)	2 (20.0%)	0 (0.0%)	1 (4.5%)	5 (8.1%)
Combined (cortical and subcortical)	5 (27.8%)	0 (0.0%)	4 (33.3%)	9 (40.9%)	18 (29.0%)

Lateralization, *n* (%)

Left	12 (66.7%)	5 (50.0%)	7 (58.3%)	8 (36.4%)	32 (51.6%)
Right	4 (22.2%)	4 (40.0%)	3 (25.0%)	11 (50.0%)	22 (35.5%)
Bilateral	2 (11.1%)	1 (10.0%)	2 (16.7%)	3 (13.6%)	8 (12.9%)

Size of infarct, *n* (%)

Large	4 (22.2%)	1 (10.0%)	1 (8.3%)	3 (13.6%)	9 (14.5%)

Small	1 (5.6%)	0 (0.0%)	0 (0.0%)	4 (18.2%)	5 (8.1%)
Unknown	13 (72.2%)	9 (90.0%)	11 (91.7%)	15 (68.2%)	48 (77.4%)

Education, *n* (%)

Specialized School	6 (33.3%)	2 (20.0%)	2 (16.7%)	3 (13.6%)	13 (21.0%)
Normal School	12 (66.7%)	8 (80.0%)	10 (83.3%)	19 (86.4%)	49 (79.0%)
- High School	0 (0.0%)	0 (0.0%)	1 (8.3%)	3 (13.6%)	4 (6.5%)

Note. VZV, varicella zoster virus; ADHD, attention deficit and hyperactivity disorder; TBI, traumatic brain injury

Appendix B. KIDSCREEN-27 questionnaire (self-rating)

Datum _____ _____

Monat   Jahr

Hallo!

Wie geht es dir? Wie fühlst du dich? Das möchten wir von dir wissen.

Bitte lies jede Frage genau durch. Was kommt dir als Antwort zuerst in den Sinn? Wähle den Kreis aus, der am besten zu deiner Antwort passt, und kreuze ihn an.

Übrigens: Das ist keine Prüfung! Du kannst also nichts falsch machen. Wichtig ist aber, dass du möglichst alle Fragen beantwortest und dass deine Kreuze gut zu sehen sind. Bitte denke dabei an die letzte Woche, also an die letzten sieben Tage.

Du musst deinen Fragebogen niemandem zeigen. Und niemand, der dich kennt, schaut deinen Fragebogen nachher an.

Zuerst ein paar Fragen zu dir selbst

Bist du weiblich oder männlich?

O weiblich

O männlich

Wie alt bist du?

_____ Jahre

Hast du eine andauernde Erkrankung oder Behinderung?

O Nein

O Ja   Welche? _____

1. Deine Gesundheit und Bewegung

1. Wie würdest du deine Gesundheit im Allgemeinen beschreiben?

O ausgezeichnet

O sehr gut

O gut

O weniger gut

O schlecht

Wenn du an die letzten Wochen denkst...

		Überhaupt nicht	Ein wenig	Mittelmässig	Ziemlich	Sehr
2.	Hast du dich fit und wohl gefühlt?	O	O	O	O	O
3.	Hast du dich viel bewegt (z.B. beim Rennen, Klettern, Velofahren)?	O	O	O	O	O
4.	Hast du gut rennen können?	O	O	O	O	O

Wenn du an letzte Woche denkst...

		Nie	Selten	Manchmal	Oft	Immer
5.	Bist du voller Energie gewesen?	O	O	O	O	O

2. Deine Gefühle und Stimmungen

Wenn du an letzte Woche denkst...

	Überhaupt nicht	Ein wenig	Mittelmässig	Ziemlich	Sehr
1. Hat dir dein Leben gefallen?	O	O	O	O	O

Wenn du an letzte Woche denkst...

	Nie	Selten	Manchmal	Oft	Immer
2. Hast du gute Laune gehabt?	O	O	O	O	O
3. Hast du Spass gehabt?	O	O	O	O	O

Wenn du an letzte Woche denkst...

	Nie	Selten	Manchmal	Oft	Immer
4. Hast du dich traurig gefühlt?	O	O	O	O	O

47

		nie	selten	al manchm	oft	immer
5.	Hast du dich so schlecht gefühlt, dass du gar nichts machen wolltest?	O	O	O	O	O
6.	Hast du dich einsam gefühlt?	O	O	O	O	O
7.	Bist du zufrieden gewesen, so wie du bist?	O	O	O	O	O

3. Familie und Freizeit

Wenn du an die letzte Woche denkst...

		nie	selten	al manchm	oft	immer
1.	Hast du genug Zeit für dich selbst gehabt?	O	O	O	O	O
2.	Hast du in deiner Freizeit die Dinge machen können, die du tun wolltest?	O	O	O	O	O
3.	Haben deine Mutter / dein Vater genug Zeit für dich gehabt?	O	O	O	O	O
4.	Haben deine Mutter / dein Vater dich gerecht behandelt?	O	O	O	O	O

5.	Hast du mit deiner Mutter / deinem Vater reden können, wenn du wolltest?	O	O	O	O	O
6.	Hast du genug Geld gehabt, um das Gleiche zu machen wie deine Freunde?	O	O	O	O	O
7.	Hast du genug Geld gehabt für die Sachen, die du brauchst?	O	O	O	O	O

4. Freunde

Wenn du an die letzte Woche denkst...

		nie	selten	al	manchm	oft	immer
1.	Hast du Zeit mit deinen Freunden verbracht?	O	O	O	O	O
2.	Hast du mit deinen Freunden Spass gehabt?	O	O	O	O	O
3.	Haben du und deine Freunde euch gegenseitig geholfen?	O	O	O	O	O

4. Hast du dich auf deine Freunde verlassen können? ○   ○   ○   ○   ○

5. Schule und Lernen

Wenn du an die letzte Woche denkst...

	überhaupt nicht	ein wenig	mittelmässig	ziemlich	sehr
1. Bist du in der Schule glücklich gewesen?	○	○	○	○	○
2. Bist du in der Schule gut zurechtgekommen?	○	○	○	○	○

Wenn du an die letzte Woche denkst...

	nie	selten	manchmal	oft	immer
3. Hast du gut aufpassen können?	○	○	○	○	○

Bist du gut mit deinen					
4. Lehrerinnen und Lehrern ausgekommen?	O	O	O	O	O

Printed in Germany
by Amazon Distribution
GmbH, Leipzig